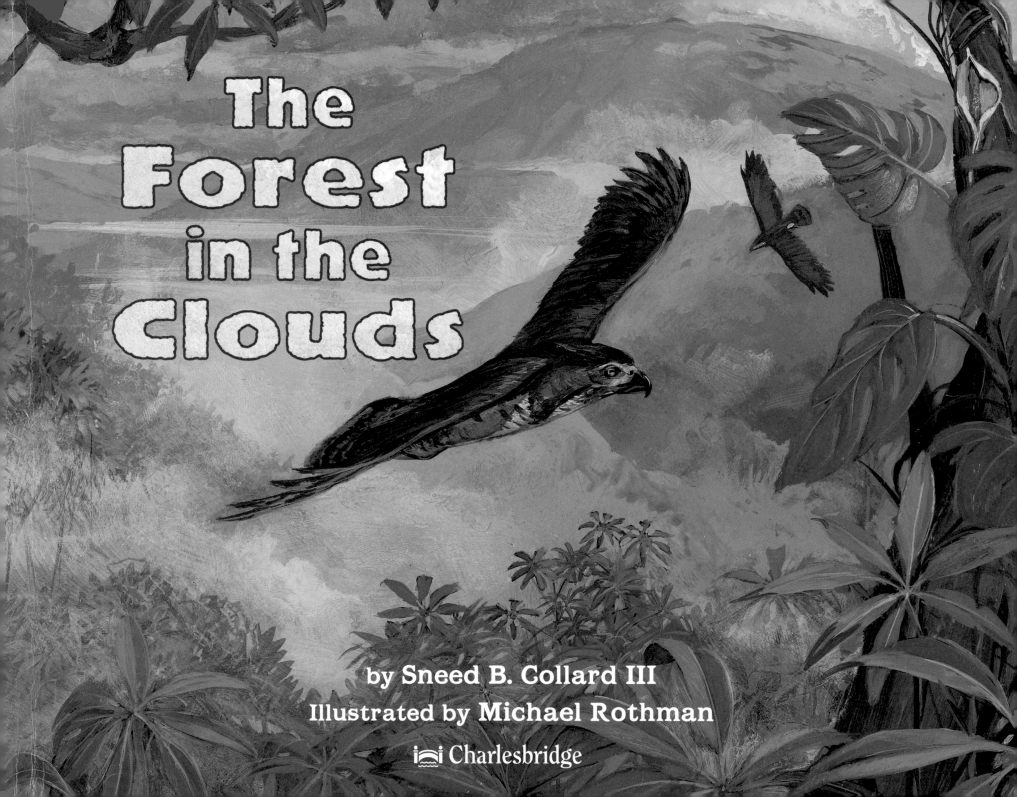

The Forest in the Clouds

by Sneed B. Collard III

Illustrated by Michael Rothman

Charlesbridge

*For Amy, who keeps my heart
in the clouds. With love,
—S.B.C. III*

*To my wife, Dorothy, and daughter, Nyanza.
—M.R.*

*Michael Rothman wishes to thank Ms. Carol
Gracie, Dr. William Haber, Dr. John Mickel,
Dr. Robbin Moran, Dr. Nalini Nadkarni, and
Dr. Adrienne Nicotra for their assistance.*

*Charlesbridge thanks Dr. Nalini Nadkarni for her
comments on text and illustrations.*

Text copyright © 2000 by Sneed Collard III
Illustrations copyright © 2000 by Michael Rothman

Published by Charlesbridge Publishing
85 Main Street, Watertown, MA 02472
(617) 926-0329
www.charlesbridge.com

Library of Congress Cataloging-in-Publication Data
Collard, Sneed B.
    The forest in the clouds/ Sneed Collard III; illustrated by
Michael Rothman.
       p.   cm.
Summary: describes some of the exotic plants and animals
that live in the cloud forest of Costa Rica, and discusses some
environmental threats faced by this region.
    ISBN 0-88106-985-X (reinforced for library use)
    ISBN 0-88106-986-8 (softcover)
1. Cloud forest ecology—Costa Rica—Reserva del Bosque
Nuboso de Monteverde—Juvenile literature.
(1. Cloud forests. 2. Cloud forest ecology. 3. Monteverde Cloud
Forest Preserve (Costa Rica))
I. Rothman, Michael, ill. II. Title.
QH108.C6C64   1999
577.34'097286'6—dc21   98-6150
                                               CIP AC
Printed in the United States of America
(hc) 10 9 8 7 6 5 4 3 2 1
(sc) 10 9 8 7 6 5 4 3 2 1

Illustrations done in acrylic paint on
3-ply Strathmore plate Bristol paper
Display type and text type set in Barcelona
Color separations made by Eastern Rainbow, Derry, N.H.
Printed and bound by Worzalla Publishing Company,
Stevens Point, Wisconsin
Production supervision by Brian G. Walker
Designed by Diane M. Earley
Printed on recycled paper

From east to west the tropical *trade winds* blow, sucking up moisture like dry, thirsty lungs from the warm Caribbean Sea. After traveling thousands of miles, these warm, wet winds strike land. They rush over the lowlands and then begin to climb.

Up and up the winds climb, cooling as they rise higher and higher. As they cool, the moisture in the winds is squeezed out of them. Tiny water droplets stick together. By the time the winds reach the top of the mountains, thick clouds have formed. This is the home of one of Earth's most enchanting places—the *tropical cloud forest*.

Bromeliad

Paddle-leaf ferns

Shoestring ferns

Ornate hawkeagle

Schefflera

Hawkmoth

American
redstart

Chlorophonia

Spangle-cheek
tanager

Purple-throated mountain gem

Scintillant hummingbird

Tropical cloud forests grow in several regions of the world and provide homes for thousands of different plants and animals. Here in the cloud forests of Costa Rica, you can find three hundred different kinds of birds. Sit quietly and you'll see over two dozen kinds of hummingbirds zoom through the cloud forest. *Mixed flocks* of redstarts, thrushes, wrens, and tanagers whirl by like little tornadoes, stirring up feasts of grasshoppers, moths, and other insects. Hunting together helps the birds catch more food—and keep a better watch for forest-falcons and other predators.

"BONK! BONK!"

A male three-wattled bellbird calls for a mate. Its bold white-and-brown colors and showy wattles tell a female, "Choose me!" Once mating is over, the shy female slips away to nest and raise her young on her own.

That flash of red, white, and green is the cloud forest's "best-dressed" bird— the resplendent quetzal. Aztecs once used the quetzals' brilliant feathers to decorate uniforms and costumes. Today thousands of tourists travel from all over the world to glimpse these dazzling creatures.

Both bellbirds and quetzals spend part of the year looking for food in lowland forests. Quetzals forage on the lower slopes and hills of the mountain range. Bellbirds and quetzals often fly hundreds of miles to forests along the Caribbean and Pacific coasts.

Each March or April the quetzals and bellbirds fly back up to the cloud forest to mate and raise their young. It is a time of abundance. Fig trees and wild avocados burst with fruit that the birds and their babies eat. Unlike most other birds, bellbirds and quetzals have big mouths, which allow them to swallow wild avocados whole.

Brown-hooded parrots

Fig tree

Resplendent
quetzal

Three-wattled
bellbird

Wild
avocado

Lobster claw

Violet sabrewing hummingbird

Metal-mark butterfly

Black-breasted wood quail

Morpho butterfly

Clearwing butterfly

None of the cloud forest plants or animals could survive without the clouds. They are the source of all life here. They drop ten *feet* of rain and mist every year, and water more than twenty-five hundred kinds of plants—including ferns, wild coffee plants, "lobster claws," and impressive "elephant ears" with six-foot leaves.

The many different kinds of flowering plants attract over five hundred species of butterflies. Some live in the cloud forest all year long, but over half are *migrants*. Like bellbirds and quetzals, they spend part of the year in lowland forests. When it becomes too dry or their food plants stop flowering, the butterflies migrate up to the wetter cloud forest or to forests on the other side of the mountain range.

Climb a one-hundred-foot fig tree and you might find a tayra hunting in the gardens of plants called *epiphytes*. Epiphytes, also called "air plants," are plants that live on other plants without harming them. More kinds of epiphytes live in the cloud forest than in any other place on Earth. Thick mats of ferns, orchids, mosses, and other epiphytes cover tree branches and trunks.

The epiphytes survive by filtering or catching water and *nutrients* from passing clouds and mist.

Tayra

Norantea costaricensis
(an epiphyte)

Tayra

Guzmania sanguinea
bromeliad (an epiphyte)

Over seventy different kinds of birds visit epiphytes to find food and building materials for their nests. Poke around the epiphyte gardens and you'll find frogs, salamanders, and thousands of beetles, ants, and other insects. Thousands of microscopic organisms also swim about in the tiny pools of water that collect in bromeliads and other epiphytes.

Mexican mouse opossum

Tree frog

Arboreal salamander

Agra beetle

Ochraceous wren

This handsome cat is a margay. The margay lives mostly in the trees, where it hunts monkeys, birds, and lizards. Few people ever see a margay. That's no accident. Many cloud forest animals play a very serious game of "hide-and-hunt." For a margay, staying hidden probably helps it sneak up on animals it is hunting. For other animals, staying hidden keeps them from *being* hunted.

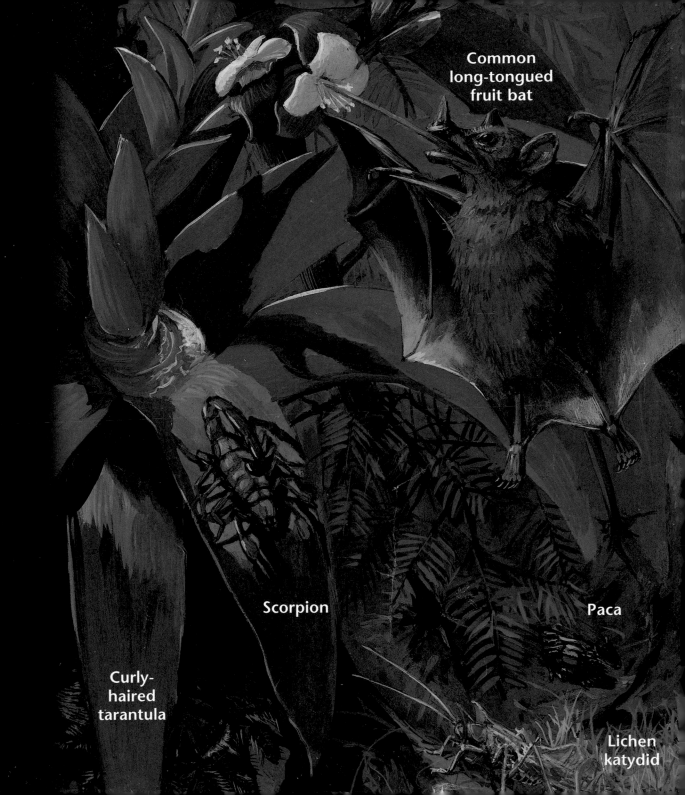

Different animals play hide-and-hunt in different ways. *Nocturnal* animals hide during the day and then come out at night. The margay is a nocturnal animal. So are the forty-three kinds of bats that fly through the nighttime woods here. Shine a flashlight and you'll catch the shining eyes of tarantulas, katydids, pacas, scorpions, walkingsticks, and many other nocturnal creatures.

Common long-tongued fruit bat

Scorpion

Paca

Curly-haired tarantula

Lichen katydid

Mexican
porcupine

Bamboo

Big fruit-eating bat

Two-toed sloth

Dink frog

Treehoppers

Highland
tinamou

Vine snake

Lizard

Brown
leaf mimic

Small-eared shrew

Camouflage hides other animals. Camouflage shapes, patterns, and colors help animals blend into their surroundings. Look carefully. Can you tell which camouflaged animals are *predators* and which are prey?

When you reach the highest point in the cloud forest—a mile above sea level— damp clouds constantly rush past. Even when it's not raining, mist makes everything dripping wet. Squeezing a moss-covered branch is like squeezing a soaked sponge; icy water trickles down your arm.

The forest here is called the *elfin forest*. Trees in the elfin forest grow only ten to twenty feet high, but they aren't short by nature. They are stunted by the constant winds howling past. Their tough branches and low profile keep these trees from being blown off the mountain.

One of the cloud forest's most mysterious residents used to live in the elfin forest—the golden toad. Scientists didn't even discover the golden toad until 1963. For most of the year the toads stayed hidden underground and under dead leaves. For a few days each rainy season, however, buckets of golden toads would mysteriously gather in shallow pools of rainwater. In the pools the toads mated and laid strings of slippery eggs. Then they disappeared until the next rainy season.

In 1988, though, the golden toads disappeared for good. Scientists searched everywhere, but they never again found the toads. No one is sure what happened to them. Some people think that pesticides in the clouds killed the toads. Scientists have also found evidence that global warming has made the cloud forest drier. These drier conditions may have weakened the toads and made them more vulnerable to deadly diseases.

The golden toads weren't the only cloud forest creatures that were harmed at this time. Twenty other species of frogs and toads, including the handsome harlequin frog, disappeared from many areas of the cloud forest. Many kinds of snakes that ate the frogs also vanished. Now some of these animals are again increasing in numbers, but not the golden toad.

The disappearance of the mysterious golden toad shows that every place on Earth is connected. Winds can carry poisonous pesticides from lowland farms to the cloud forest many miles away. Pollution from power plants and cars can disrupt the weather all over the world. Despite these kinds of problems, people are working hard to protect the Earth's natural places, including the cloud forest.

Some work to buy land to set aside for cloud forest plants and animals. Others work with nearby farmers to plant trees that help to provide food for quetzals and other birds. Others educate the public about all the good things that forests do for us—things such as making oxygen, keeping the soil from washing away, and providing us with medicines.

Children all over the world are helping, too.
Kids from Sweden all the way to Australia have helped raise money
to protect the cloud forest. To find out how you can help, write to:

The Children's Rainforest
P.O. Box 936
Lewiston, ME 04243

The Monteverde Institute
Apartado 10165
Monteverde, Puntarenas
Costa Rica

The Nature Conservancy
International Children's Rainforest Program
1815 North Lynn Street
Arlington, VA 22209

Books

The following books offer additional information about Costa Rica's
cloud forest and about tropical forests in general:

Children Save the Rain Forest by Dorothy Hinshaw Patent. Published by Cobblehill Books, 1996.

Monteverde: Science and Scientists in a Costa Rican Cloud Forest by Sneed B. Collard III.
Published by Franklin Watts, 1997.

At Home in the Rain Forest by Diane Willow. Published by Charlesbridge Publishing, 1991.

The Most Beautiful Roof in the World by Kathryn Lasky. Published by Harcourt Brace, 1997.

Web Sites

http://www.evergreen.edu/monteverde
(Monteverde: Ecology and Conservation of a Tropical Cloud Forest)

http://www.monteverde.or.cr/
(The Monteverde Conservation League)

Two other sites provide excellent information about rain forest conservation
and include links to many other rain forest- and environment-related sites.

http://www.ran.org/
(The site for the Rainforest Action Network)

http://www.wri.org/wri/
(The site for the World Resources Institute)

About the Cloud Forest in This Book

Cloud forests exist in many parts of the world, including Africa, Asia, South and Central America, Hawaii, and the Caribbean. Each cloud forest is different and special in its own way. The cloud forest in this book is located in the mountains near the town of Monteverde, Costa Rica. Here, a large preserve protects over seventy-five thousand acres of forest for plants, animals, and people.

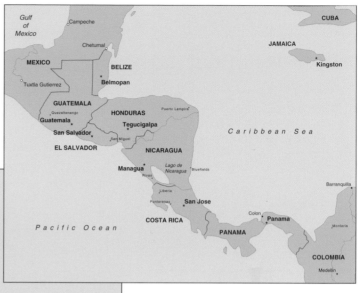

NICARAGUA

Liberia

Nicoya

Alajuela

★ San Jose

• Puntarenas

Caribbean Sea

Trade Winds

• Puerto Limón

Puerto Quepos

• San Isidro

COSTA RICA

Golfito

PANAMA

Pacific Ocean

MONTEVERDE CLOUD FOREST

One Mile

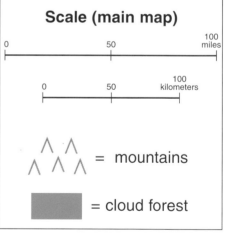

Scale (main map)

0   50   100 miles

0   50   100 kilometers

⋀ ⋀ ⋀
⋀ ⋀ ⋀ ⋀ = mountains

█ = cloud forest

Map sources used: MapArt by Cartesia Software, World Conservation Monitoring Centre, David King, and a standard atlas.

Glossary

camouflage—colors or shapes of an animal or plant that make it hard to detect by other animals.

elfin forest—part of a cloud forest where the plants are stunted by constant exposure to wind.

epiphytes (EH-PIH-FITES)—"air plants" that live on the branches, trunks, or leaves of other plants, getting support, but not nutrients, from their hosts.

migrants—animals such as birds or butterflies that regularly travel long distances from one place to another, usually in search of food or nesting sites.

mixed flocks—different species of birds that hunt or forage together in groups.

nocturnal—animals that are active mostly or entirely at night.

nutrient—a chemical or compound that plants and animals need to grow and stay healthy. Common nutrients include nitrogen and phosphorus.

predator—any organism that survives by capturing and eating animals.

trade wind—a wind that blows almost continually in the same direction.

tropical cloud forest—a high-altitude forest watered by a steady stream of clouds and rainfall during much of the year. Also called a *tropical montane forest*.